ENDORSEMENTS FOR *CATTLE, CROPS, AND SPURS: DOING BUSINESS THE COWBOY WAY*

"Dr. Gobeille has provided an insightful guidepost for us all—the cowboy way. In a world lacking true leadership and real values, he makes a strong case for living a principles-based life."

Knute Buehler, MD
Orthopedic Surgeon
Representative, Oregon House
of Representatives

"Dave's book and Dave's life are vivacious and virtuous. He exemplifies virtue, enthusiasm, and a zest for living. He is the kind of cowboy I'd want to be if I were a cowboy. *Cattle, Crops, and Spurs: Doing Business the Cowboy Way* is a celebration, a challenge, and a confirmation. It's a celebration of a life that is simple and rich. It's a cogent challenge to readers to be people of character. It's a confirmation that God is a God of love, a God who comes to us and speaks our language. He not only came to us, He became one of us. When He comes to cowboys He doesn't wear a robe and sandals, He wears a cowboy hat, and dusty, dirty blue jeans. Thanks

Dave, for challenging us to live by the Cowboy Code, the Golden Rule, and the Ten Commandments."

Ken Johnson
Pastor Emeritus, Westside
Church, Bend, Oregon
Author of *Life Squared:*
The Secret to Limitless Living

"I have known Dave Gobeille for forty years and know him to be one of my greatest mentors and a man of character. *Cattle, Crops, and Spurs: Doing Business the Cowboy Way* is a book that should be read by all businessmen. Living life by the principles in this book would make this a better world for all of us. I strongly encourage you to read it and digest what is on its pages. You will be better for it."

Steve Johnson
Businessman
Defensive End for the Denver
Gold (USFL)

"Dave's parables and insights of life's greatest commandments, with his humanism references, are a testament to his business acumen and leadership from a servant's heart.

"This compact read is an inspirational and entertaining guide for anyone aspiring to a higher level, no matter what your career or station in life."

David Niles
Successful Orthodontist
Creator of a Debt-Free Lifestyle
Coaching Mentor

"I would encourage every businessperson to read *Cattle, Crops, and Spurs: Doing Business the Cowboy Way*. It does not matter if you are just starting out, or an older seasoned warrior. So many key concepts presented with unique illustrations, making it impossible to miss the points! It touches on 'the good life' and long-term success, and concepts important and universal to achieving these life goals. So many important business principles, habits for success, and essential values presented in great, entertaining, pull-me-into-the-moment stories and experiences. Dave's ability to teach and, at the same time, captivate the reader, is a true gift. This is probably one of the best-written business books I have read in several years."

Pete Pifer
Successful Serial Entrepreneur
The Leading Ground Gaining
Fullback at Oregon State University

CATTLE, CROPS, AND SPURS:

Doing Business the Cowboy Way

2 Timothy 1:7
"Have no fear"

By
David M. Gobeille

David M. Gobeille

Deep River
BOOKS

ISBN – 13: 9781632694492
Library of Congress: 2017945073
Illustrations by Stefanie Crowe
Printed in the USA
Cover design by Joe Bailen, Contajus Designs

TABLE OF CONTENTS

ACKNOWLEDGMENTS AND DEDICATION

This book is dedicated to my gorgeous wife of forty-nine years. Carolyn is definitely my completion and my greatest joy. In addition, my sons Matthew and Todd have brought me more pleasure than a man deserves. Each one has taught me more about the Lord and has helped to change my life, and continues to do so. My grandchildren Madeline, Amelia, and Alonzo are the absolute joy of my life. They are the main reason I have written this book. I pray for them every day and ask God to protect them, help them make good Godly decisions, and draw each one into deep intimate relationship with Himself. I also pray He will guide them to the one who will be their completion for their lives. I know that He is preparing that person for each one of them. Since I have a lifetime of information in my brain, I'm likely not sure of where each tidbit is from. I apologize for not giving credit to everyone who has had a profound influence on my life.

Most of all, praise be to the God of the universe. Without His leadership in my life, I would be "nothing but a filthy rag."

PREFACE

How can a young man cleanse his way?
By taking heed according to Your word.
With my whole heart I have sought You;
Oh, let me not wander from Your commandments!
Your word I have hidden in my heart,
That I might not sin against You.
Blessed are you, O Lord!
Teach me Your statutes.
With my lips I have declared
All the judgments of Your mouth.
I have rejoiced in the way of Your testimonies.
As much as in all riches.
I will meditate on Your precepts,
And contemplate Your ways.
I will delight myself in Your statutes;
I will not forget Your word. (Ps. 119:9–16)

King David wrote:

Why do the nations rage,
And the people plot a vain thing?
The kings of the earth set themselves,
And the rulers take counsel together,
Against the Lord and against His Anointed. (Ps. 2:1–2)

The world is starved for leadership and people of integrity. In almost every area of American life today, we see failure for people to act with integrity. On Wall Street (representing the business world), in government (local, state, and federal), and in the news reports about the everyday lives of Americans, we see moral failure and a loss of the ideals that made this country great.

Of course, it is inappropriate to generalize, and there are many people of character who make up our country. Leadership with character, however, is sadly lacking all across the land.

I believe that character is not something that can be made up or improvised. Having standards by which we live our lives must start with absolutes established by God. Does that mean that leaders must all be perfect? No, it does not. Nonetheless, as J. Oswald Sanders once pointed out, when people who lack "spiritual fitness" are placed in a position of leadership, God quietly withdraws and leaves them to implement their own policies according to their own standards, but without His aid. The result is a failure to lead with true character.[1]

We live in a country that was founded on spiritual values. Some call it the "Judeo-Christian" ethic. Although our founding fathers were not perfect, they seemed to have one thing in mind. A country with checks and balances, and, a focus on guiding character values.

In my life experience, following God's truth is the way to a life of peace and fulfillment. God has delivered to us truth and grace—an unusual paradox. When we begin to understand this, life becomes far more manageable and leads to greater success. Success is elusive for many of us because it is so misunderstood. Success in God's economy is much different than in our frame of reference. I've learned that success can be measured by how much peace we have in every situation. God says for us to "not be conformed to this world, but to be transformed by the renewing of your minds, that you may prove what is that good and acceptable and perfect will of God" (Rom. 12:2). You see, being in God's will is what brings us peace in all situations. God's Word also says, "in everything give thanks; for this is the will of God in Christ Jesus for you" (1 Thess. 5:18). That means in *everything*. And we know "all things work together for those who love God, to those who are the called according to His purpose" (Rom. 8:28). That means *all* things, not just the good and pleasurable things.

In my life, the people who demonstrate the truth of this Scripture are the cowboys I've known. Their lives are often living examples of these truths, and it can be seen in their everyday activities. As a result, I felt it would be good to take a look at business and leadership in that context. *Cattle, Crops, and Spurs: Doing Business the Cowboy Way* is the result of that effort.

What I write about here are principles I have learned throughout my life. As I've taken examples from my cowboy life and the lives of other cowboys I've had the privilege of knowing, you will see that the great American cowboy can give us examples of life lived with some peace in all circumstances.

Someone once said that there are no new ideas. All ideas are passed along in one way or another. Hopefully what I share is God-given. When I know the source, I've tried to give credit.

My hope is that you will see truth and grace played out in a "real world way."

CHAPTER 1

WHY THE COWBOY WAY?

Somewhere along the way, we became lost. There is one American icon who seems to represent those original values. That is the American Cowboy. The almost mythical character of the cowboy is what drives this book.

Badger Clark wrote a poem called "A Cowboy's Prayer" that gives a flavor of the character of the people who have represented all that is good about our country:

Oh Lord, I've never lived where churches grow.
     I love creation better as it stood
That day You finished it so long ago
     And looked upon Your work and called it good.
I know that others find you in the light
     That's sifted down through tinted window panes,

And yet I seem to feel You near tonight
    In this dim, quiet starlight on the plains

I thank you Lord, that I am placed so well,
    That You have made my freedom so complete;
That I'm no slave of whistle, clock or bell,
    Nor weak eyed prisoner of wall and street.
Just let me live my life as I've begun
    And give me work that's open to the sky,
Make me a pardner of the wind and sun,
    And I won't ask a life that's soft or high.

Let me be easy on the man that's down;
    Let me be square and generous with all.
I'm careless sometimes, Lord, when I'm in town,
    But never let 'em say I'm mean or small!
Make me as big and open as the plains,
    As honest as the hoss between my knees,
Clean as the wind that blows behind the rains,
    Free as the hawk that circles on the breeze!

Forgive me, Lord, if sometimes I forget.
    You know about the reasons that are hid.
You understand the things that gall and fret;
    You know me better than my mother did.
Just keep an eye on all that's done and said,
    And right me when I sometimes turn aside,
And guide me on the long, dim, trail ahead
    That stretches upward toward the Great Divide.

The heart of the cowboy can be felt in that poem. Many decisions have to be made, life is hard, and God will provide. The cowboy has freedom *with* responsibility, and he will get the job done with pride and a great work ethic. He's a self-manager, totally responsible for his actions, and he is generous and kind as well as tough and courageous. Times can be hard and the cowboy sometimes makes mistakes, but in the end, he knows where to turn for the perfect answers, and does so with integrity.

J. Oswald Sanders said, "More failure comes from an excess of caution than from bold experiments with new ideas." He also said, "Successful leaders have learned that no failure is final, whether his own failure or someone else's. No one is perfect, and we cannot be right all the time. Failures and even feelings of inadequacy can provoke humility and serve to remind a leader who is really in charge."[2] These are things that cowboys know all too well.

The cowboy was instrumental in developing the West, and most had a good idea of who was really in charge. And I believe they exemplify people with enthusiasm, energy, a zest for life, *and* humility, all at the same time.

Their lives were not easy. They battled the "elements" in every sense of the word. Severe weather conditions, long droughts, hostile Indians, wild horses, cows and other wild animals, range and land disputes, fencing issues, poverty, personal and animal illnesses, and unbelievably long working hours and other hardships were their reality. Yet, they learned how to work, improvise, and survive in the harshest of conditions. There is certainly no "quit" in the cowboy.

And in all of those circumstances, they learned to trust others and contracted with people using a smile and a handshake. They knew how to have fun and enjoy their lives, alongside an unflappable work ethic. In a "pinch" they knew where their strength needed to come from. The cowboy was known as a man with a simple faith and the humility to trust God, even though many cowboys are not particularly "religious."

Let's journey together, to see how we, too, can become people of character like the legendary cowboy.

What does it mean to do business the cowboy way? What are the characteristics we can look to that we may live a rich life, well lived? What are the growth-restricting obstacles that keep us from being people of character and integrity?

I have had the privilege of being a part-time cowboy a significant part of my adult life. I have had a passion for horses. Cows and hay are part of our income stream. I live on a small ranch in the high desert of Central Oregon, and every day I count it a privilege to see how the things I do teach me "the way to go." I have competed in rodeos and have shown rope horses at American Quarter Horse Association competitions. I have worked our cattle and often ridden in the wilderness. I have had experiences many men will never have. I've learned to be courageous in spite of fear. I've learned to be found, when I was completely lost. I've learned to plant seed that seems "dead" and watched as God's plan brought it to life to feed livestock and pay ranch bills. I've spent more hours on a tractor than I can count, giving me wonderful opportunities to reflect on life and God's plan. I have truly been baptized in the way of the cowboy. I don't speak of cowboy things in a philosophical way. These are the things that I have had the privilege to live out, and observe in other cowboys. These experiences have taught me some of life's greatest lessons. These experiences and many others in my life give me a platform to speak into the lives of other men as a certified executive and business coach.

What is the cowboy code, or as some call it, the code of the West? This was not a written code. Imagine, if you will, living in a primitive land with no actual laws. Imagine a person, primarily coming to this land for adventure and to seek a fortune in the new frontier. In situations like this it would be easy for anarchy to rule the land. But people in the early West developed a code of living, which was appropriate for keeping some "moral order" in this wild frontier. It was also important for their survival. They needed to be in positive relationship with others to survive.

This code became universal enough that many people have written about it over the years in novels and western mythology of all sorts. However, this code was not myth, but developed out of the tough life to be lived in the early West. Ramon F. Adams wrote:

> Back in the days when the cowman and his herds made a new frontier there wasn't much law on the range. Lack of written law made it necessary for 'im to frame some of his own, so he developed a rule of behavior that became a kind of code of the West. Them homespun laws, bein' merely a gentleman's agreement to certain rules of conduct for survival, were never wrote into the statutes, but became respected ever'where on the range nevertheless.[3]

By the 1950s, many of the day's movies and movie stars exemplified this "code." Many of these early "western heroes" wrote what they knew to be the "code" from their points of view. For example, Gene Autry's Code of Honor:

1. A cowboy never takes unfair advantage—even of an enemy.
2. A cowboy never betrays a trust. He never goes back on his word.
3. A cowboy always tells the truth.
4. A cowboy is kind and gentle to small children, old folks, and animals.

5. A cowboy is free from racial and religious intolerances.
6. A cowboy is always helpful when someone is in trouble.
7. A cowboy is always a good worker.
8. A cowboy respects womanhood, his parents, and his nation's laws.
9. A cowboy is clean about his person in thought, word, and deed.
10. A cowboy is a patriot.

In addition, cowboys writing codes/creeds included Hopalong Cassidy's "Creed for American Boys and Girls," Roy Rogers's "Rider Club Rules," and the Texas Rangers' "Deputy Ranger" Oath. Many have written what they believe were the unwritten code of rules for the early cowboy to live by.

God, of course, also gave us a code of conduct, and when written the "cowboy way" it would look like this:

COWBOY TEN COMMANDMENTS

1. Just one God.
2. Honor your Pa and Ma.
3. No telling tales or gossipin'.
4. Git yourself to Sunday meeting.
5. Put nothing before God.
6. No fooling around with another cowboy's gal.
7. No killin'.
8. Watch your mouth.
9. Don't take what ain't yours.
10. Don't be hankerin' for yer buddy's stuff.

For the purpose of this book, I have distilled all these different ideas down to a cowboy code, which applies to the operation of any business. With each "code" or "rule," I will give an example from my personal "western life" of how this has played out.

CHAPTER 2

THERE IS ALWAYS JUST ONE BOSS

A cowboy always "rode for the brand." What did that mean, and what does that mean in any business situation? The word that seems most appropriate is "loyalty."

How does loyalty manifest itself in business and life? Our first obligation is to be loyal to our Creator, our ultimate Boss. But what does that look like?

When I worked for other ranchers, as a buckaroo, it was critical that I be loyal to their vision. That vision may be his overriding philosophy for his ranch, or just his goals for that particular "day work."

I remember one fall when I was helping to guide a deer hunt for a rancher friend. His goal was to move deer in a way that would allow the hunters to have a chance to harvest one while sitting on a stand at a stationary location. He chose this method because it was the best way to have people experience a deer hunt without the risk of shooting each other. Each person was situated on a hillside in rugged country where they could not see the other hunters around them. Meanwhile, our job was to ride out and away from the hunters and then make a several-mile sweep back around toward them, in hopes that some deer would move in the direction of the hunters. I knew the land where I rode and it is "big country." I was given the assignment to take a particular route, and to start that direction at a particular time. We would only occasionally see the other cowboys during this multiple-hour ride. I knew where I was to go, and I also knew it was steep, rocky country.

As I approached the halfway point, I came to a place with only one route. It was extremely steep and narrow. With my heart in my throat, I started the climb on horseback and wondered if my horse would stumble and fall several hundred feet from that steep rocky wall.

We'll get back to our story in a minute. First, let me share a bigger concept with you.

In business, we must strive to be servant leaders. No matter what level of authority we have in business, we always have someone of higher authority over us. In that context, we must look to our Boss, as we learn to lead and serve those who are under our authority.

This one concept alone would allow the world to be a better place. In our quest to be in control, we fail to see that we are never really in control. In business, we make many decisions. When we make these decisions unilaterally, we often find that we have made disastrous mistakes. Wouldn't it be wonderful to know we can make more decisions, with less mistakes, if we follow the Real Boss?

The good news: We have only one Boss to whom we must be totally obedient. In our businesses, after we consult the Boss, we can make good decisions with the consultation of those around us.

Lest you think I am suggesting that we act like puppets, let me remind you that most businesses have an overriding vision. Often, they have developed that thought more succinctly into a mission statement. Usually, when we have wise management, they want us to make good decisions on our own volition, but in the context of their vision. The beauty in business is there are multiple correct decisions in any given circumstance. Our goal with the help of God and our fellow teammates is to make the very best decision. "Best" always supersedes "good."

Back to that treacherous ride. After I crested what was literally a cliff, I soon spied the others on horseback, and the timing was perfect for the best hunt possible. In that moment, I knew that my trust in God, and the directions of the person I had placed my trust and loyalty in, had worked out perfectly. It is so true for the cowboy life: The way is hard, but the rewards are always there at the end of the day. In addition, we can learn that courage is often measured by being afraid and following through anyway.

In the end, I managed to come out on top, exactly as I was told. In my humanness, it would have seemed appropriate to turn back. However, I trusted my friend and my horse, and knew that the obstacle was not insurmountable. It was my loyalty to his experience and integrity that allowed me to complete the trip.

It's funny that when God gives us real direction, it's oftentimes not very comfortable to follow Him, just as it was not comfortable for me to follow that trail. But in our walk with Him, it is always best to do just as He says. If I had not had that confidence, and not followed my friend's directions, I would have ruined a half-day hunt for his customers and wasted everyone else's time. In that moment, I "rode for the brand" and trusted just one Boss.

CHAPTER 3

LIVE A LIFE THAT HONORS OTHERS

Cowboys choose to honor others around themselves. Why? Survival. In a difficult and dangerous career, cowboys often must depend on each other for their very survival. If a man stopped by an old "line shack" during a long ride, he was usually offered a meal and a place to sleep. To this day, ranches frequently depend on neighboring cowboys for day work and help at times like when they are branding cattle. Cowboys from near and far will travel miles in a truck with a horse trailer to help a fellow rancher to gather cattle, or at branding time in the spring. It is common for rodeo cowboys to help each other, even though they are competing against those they help. Next time you go to a rodeo, or watch one on TV, check the behavior of the cowboys behind the chutes, as those they compete against get ready to ride.

There are many times when neighbors and friends have helped me with cattle and horses and I have traveled those miles to help out as well. On these occasions, there is an atmosphere of community, and it is often a social event. "Barn raisings" in the old days were such events, as settlers began to develop their land. I've helped at brandings and helped move cattle to different pastures or allotments. At our ranch, we have frequently had a fall "harvest" party to celebrate the end of a farming season and to thank those who have helped us.

I once read a story[4] set in 1874; a Texas rancher/cattleman named Willis McCutcheon sized up a young lad named Sol West and decided that despite his youth he'd "do" to drive the McCutcheon firm's first herd of the year to Ellsworth, Kansas. "You'll get half of whatever these cows bring over the price per head, after expenses," McCutcheon promised. The boy said that would be fine.

The drive was halfway to Ellsworth when a five-hour blizzard killed the trail crew's remuda (herd) of seventy-eight horses. Having promised to get the cattle through, West traded some cows—and with them, part of his profits—for six horses and a mule. A month later he managed to get the cattle to the Kansas market. He sold them off, a few at a time, during the summer and fall.

How does this relate to business?

Does honoring your employer or honoring your customer take first priority in your company? I once had an attorney who created a new kind of trust. After many of his clients participated in and contributed to these trusts, the IRS ruled that this was not legal under the tax code. Over the next year, he covered the cost of challenging the IRS in court and won, while at the same time returning any lost money to the clients. The dollar amount was quite large, but he honored his clients and put them first at his personal expense.

I remember one time after an elk hunt on Aldrich Mountain in a blinding snowstorm, two of us arrived back at the trail head with a string of horses. It was late and after dark and it had snowed three or four feet of powdery snow. My partner would only have one chance to get his truck and horse trailer off the mountain, or risk leaving it until spring. We decided he would get in his truck and try to "power" his way the several miles off the mountain, and I would follow with the string of horses until I found his truck at the highway that intersected with this forest service road. After he left, with a wake of flying snow coming off the front of his truck, I started off Aldrich Mountain with the string of horses. It had snowed so hard and long, and the snow was so powdery, that there were no truck tire tracks to follow. In the dark, following the "cut" in the trees, I finally reached his truck several hours later. We had both participated in a decision, which was best for the situation at hand. We each had different roles, but we honored each other's part.

Back to our story of the young cowboy. When West finally returned to Lavaca County in December, McCutcheon's bookkeeper figured the profits, deducting the value of the lost horses; West made no objection. "Are you going to buy a herd of your own, or start a bank?" the bookkeeper joked as he handed over the young man's profit: seventy-five cents. West smiled and pocketed the coins, without a complaint at the outcome of a deal that he had sealed with his word.

Is this how you do business, or is it profiting at all costs? This is a very important question to ask. Honoring your company, your supervisor, your direct reports, and, most importantly, your customers first—these will have the most lasting results. That is the lesson learned from the Code of the Cowboy.

Sometimes honoring others involves overcoming enemies of relationship and of excellence. What if someone does not feel worthy of you honoring him or her? Or, what if the other person is afraid of having a relationship with you? What if there are circumstances that make relationship difficult? To illustrate this point, I want to share a few stories that highlight what I'm talking about.

I'm reminded of a time when I went to feed cows in a particular pasture. As I entered the pasture in my ATV, I noticed a dead fawn lying in the middle of this particular field. I walked slowly over to this animal and could not detect the slightest breathing. After watching for several minutes, I called my wife on the cell phone to let her know what I had found. There seemed to be no injuries; my wife suggested that maybe it was only sick or suffering. She drove her car down and told me that she wanted me to pick the fawn up and put it in her car to drive to the veterinarian's office. That didn't seem reasonable to me, but when mamma's not happy, nobody's happy.

As I started over to pick up this fawn, I happened to look over at a stand of juniper trees; lo and behold, there was the doe, watching every move. Now I was really careful as I bent over to pick up this young deer. I no sooner picked up the fawn than the little thing let out a scream I will not soon forget. A fawn may seem small, and I am a big man, but that little thing launched out of my arms and ran straight toward his mother. The fawn was playing dead. The doe, in the meantime, was debating coming over and eating me alive. The doe and the fawn wanted no part of a relationship with me, even though my intentions were good.

This sometimes also happens in work relationships, especially between supervisors and their teams. What must one do? The most important thing is to state and clarify your intentions, and be very clear about what your motives are. Recent neuroscience tells us that we must give at least three positive communications for every effort at making corrections with your team members. You see, all communications are not solicited or welcome, and we must often learn to communicate very carefully.

From time to time we have buffalo on the ranch, for working with cutting horses. They are very durable, tough animals, and have tremendous stamina. The first time we had a buffalo at home I asked the owner about what I should do if it were to get out of its enclosure. I suggested that I should rope it and drag it back. (Buffalo cannot be confined by fences if they don't want to be; that's a story for a different time.) The owner told me that if the buffalo got out, to not rope it. The reason is that the wind pipe of a buffalo is triangular in shape, and if you rope it you are likely to cause that trachea to collapse and it will lead to suffocation. This was learned the hard way by cowboys of days gone by.

The essence of this story is to say that not all team members want to be led. There are teachable and coachable team members, and there are leaders and coaches that can coach. But that's not always the case. My philosophy is that team members should be given every opportunity to succeed until they prove they cannot be led; then a change is necessary. In the case of the buffalo escaping, the cowboy must do his best to use his horse-cutting techniques to guide the animal back to the enclosure, but that might not be possible. Most humans can be coached and led if given all the information and resources they need, and the leader should expect that they will be successful.

So you can see that living a life that honors others is the goal. The expectation is that everyone will be successful and coachable. When we try to honor others and commit ourselves to their success, we should approach it from a positive point of view, expecting great results. However, even

Jesus—the greatest teacher of all time—knew that not everyone would respond, and at one point told his disciples that if they entered a village and were not well received to "dust off their sandals" and move on. The bottom line: We need to expect people to succeed until they prove that they cannot. In business and in everyday life, honoring others always leads to greater success.

CHAPTER 4

NOTHING WORKS LIKE THE TRUTH

Are you ever concerned about inconsistencies in your code? The cowboy code includes a contractual bond of a man's word. Most "deals" in the old West—and many "deals" today among cowboys—are sealed with a smile and a handshake. In the simplest form, the code was merely a common ethic of fair play. What happened? Look where we are today.

In a funny and yet at the same time deadly story: When I first started ranching I bought two Hereford cows. I purchased them in the valley after we moved to the high desert. Within a few days one cow died of pneumonia. When people asked how the startup of ranching was going, I would jokingly tell them "I lost half my herd." Of course, they would respond in a very sympathetic way. I was able to doctor the second cow back to health. Wouldn't it have been novel if the seller had said, "The cows were infected when they left here, and I would stand by the sale. I will replace your lost cow"? That did not happen.

In another personal story, as I started to develop a hay field, with initially small yields, I decided to do an experiment. I was going to be gone from the ranch for a while and put an advertisement in the newspaper to sell the hay. When people called, I told them to go and take the hay they needed and put the money for it in a coffee can I had left by the stacks.

You guessed it: When I returned to the ranch, I found an empty coffee can, and most of the hay was gone. That pretty much sums up the state of affairs today in our culture.

As most people know, when you practice truth and justice all the time, you can't get "caught" in a lie. "Honesty" today has lots of "grey" areas—"I generally told the truth," or "I told the truth, but I just left a little bit out."

I once had a cowboy acquaintance I team roped with who was called "fairly honest Bob" (not his real name). I don't know about you, but that is not how I want to be known. The cowboy code was very simple and involved "being your word," period. How refreshing it would be if we all took a little lesson from that concept.

Cowboys of the old West were much more literal in their thought process. The bond of a man's word, the noose for the horse thief, and the obligation of hospitality for the visiting cowboy were very much a part of the code by which they lived. The rough and tumble West called out for some rules and mores, because otherwise there would have been pure chaos. If you think about it, however, if a man is "not his word" what does that leave him with? All too often, people don't understand. At the end of the day, without honesty, you have nothing. To the cowboy, honesty is absolute. If you can't "be your word," who are you?

The most amazing animal of the ranch can teach another lesson on honesty. That animal is, of course, the horse. One time, I visited some friends and they wanted to take a pleasure ride. They were from the city and had purchased a ranch for recreation. They told me that one of the horses in the small corral was uncatchable. While they continued to visit on the front porch of their cabin, I walked down to the corral and picked up a lead rope. I stepped into the corral and quietly and slowly approached the horse. I made no effort to catch the horse; I just waited patiently while he got used to me being in the same space with him. Slowly but surely, he approached me. I rubbed his neck and talked softly to him. Eventually, I placed his halter on. Like any horseman will tell you, he had just developed a lack of trust. As a result, he became uncooperative.

When we're not honest, people will react the same way with us. In business, when people find us dishonest, they become uncooperative. People in business can practice greed and dishonesty for a period of time but it will always catch up with them. It reveals to us that if we practice complete honesty and some healthy measure of transparency with those we lead, they will learn to cooperate. In this way, we can achieve much higher levels of performance. When I sell hay to my hay broker, I always practice transparency and honesty in terms of bale weights and quality of the hay. Because of environmental circumstances beyond my control such as rain, it's not always possible to guarantee perfect hay. But because I have been honest and fair, he has bought hay from me for years without any questions asked.

Unfortunately, in business many people think the Golden Rule is, "He who has the gold, rules." However, the real Golden Rule says, "Treat others the way you want them to treat you." It's all very simple. Why is it so hard for modern businessmen and -women to practice this? The result of this concept, when practiced, is win-win. The more honest you are, the more respected you are. The more respected you are, the more cooperation you get. The more cooperation you get, the more productive people become. Amen.

CHAPTER 5

GET YOURSELF TO SUNDAY
MEETING/A HEALTHY CULTURE

The cowboy has a hard life by outside standards. He works long hours, in oftentimes difficult conditions. One thing is true almost universally: Cowboys lead a simple and somewhat orderly life. We might call this part of the "cowboy culture."

In my barn, my saddles always go in the same place. My tie-downs and bridles are always on the stall with the horse that wears them day in and day out. Feed is always kept in a very neat place in order to keep it from spoiling or being invaded by rodents. When I team rope, I always ride my horse into the roping box and turn my horse toward the chute, and thus toward the cows. That way my horse develops a routine; it causes him to be more consistent. Cowboys always approach the horse the same way, and get on and off on the same side. Working cowboy tools such as saddles, chaps, and reins are always taken care of—especially the leather ones. Cowboys move cattle in an orderly, quiet way whenever possible. They make sure the animals are fed each day and usually at the same time. They are vigilant about the health of each animal; they know every cow and horse, and in most cases they know them by their behavior patterns, even their ear tag number and name if they have given them one. That is true even if they have five hundred head of cattle. They are very observant and aware of their environment, including potential changes in weather and other conditions.

When I ride in the mountains with other cowboys, especially before and after major weather patterns, I am vigilant to note every possible landmark and to notice even the smallest things, in order to not get disoriented or lost. One time, years ago, I took my sister for a horse pack camping trip in the Three Sisters Wilderness area. We had two horses to ride and I took a packhorse for our camping gear. My sister was not an experienced rider, so I made sure she had a very gentle horse and focused on safety every step of the way. Life in the mountains often becomes very unpredictable from the start.

Life is very unpredictable as well. When I coach businesspeople, my goal is to help them seek order, develop goals, and prepare action steps. These are all part of a life of excellence. Many people, however, seem to float along through life without much effort to keep order and balance.

When I start the coaching process with business clients, we often talk about the "7 Fs" in their lives. Those areas are Faith, Family, Friends, Fitness, Fun, Finances, and Future. If any of these areas in their lives are "out of order," they will not be able to live at the level of excellence that is possible. I will ask them to create a "vision statement" for each of the seven areas, and to develop action steps to intentionally work toward that vision. Some clients have specific areas that need to be worked on, and some clients have never addressed any of these areas. The usual result for those clients is that their lives are in sad repair. The coaching I do helps them work through these areas and come up with their own answers to some of the issues that might prevent them from living lives of excellence.

This is very much like the cowboy. He has many things come his way each and every day. No two days are alike. Does that sound familiar? His job, at times, is to keep order in the midst of chaos. Sometimes, however, one must restore order out of emergency situations. That calls for very intentional living.

Let me get back to the story of the horse-packing trip with my sister. We hauled the horses up to Foley Ridge Trail-head by horse trailer on a beautiful late August day. The weather was warm and the sky was blue. You could smell the pine forest as we unloaded the horses and saddled them. I put our gear on my packhorse, and I tied a diamond hitch to secure the load. We started off on the trail into the wilderness area. We weren't a hundred yards down the trail when, with me in the lead and without knowing it, I rode over a yellow jacket nest with my horse and the packhorse. Of course, by the time my sister reached the spot in the trail, the yellow jackets were really stirred up. They began to sting her horse— and that was the beginning of a small rodeo. Remember, my sister was not an experienced rider, and I was way ahead of her on my horse, with the lead rope of the packhorse in my right hand. The unexpected often delivers trouble.

All I could do is holler at her to spur her horse and ride ahead as quickly as possible. I had to deliver the "message" in a firm way, but did not want to spook the other horses and hers as well. Fortunately, she followed my directions and "crow-hopped" down the trail. I was able to grab her reins, and we finally got the situation under control. The rest of the ten-to-twelve-mile ride in was uneventful, and we eventually made camp in Deception Creek Meadow. The rest of the day was beautiful, and my Dutch oven camp cooking wasn't bad either.

We slept well, but when we woke up in the morning I took one look at the sky and knew we were in trouble. It was not normal to snow that time of year in the mountains, but I knew snow clouds when I saw them. I told my sister we were going to pack up immediately. She was hesitant and wanted to know why. I told her she would see very soon. By the time we packed up camp and saddled the horses, it had started to snow—I don't mean a "White Christmas" snow; I mean a blinding snowstorm. By the time we reached the trailhead at the edge of the meadow, fifty yards from where we had camped, it was a whiteout. I knew the trail well. The only problem was, I couldn't see it.

What every good cowboy knows, however, is that horses have a very keen sense of direction. With a little coaxing from me, and the incredible sense of our horses, we arrived at the truck and horse trailer a few hours later. With a little shot of whiskey to warm us up, my sister agreed it was one of her life's great adventures. She has had many, like climbing Mt. Rainier and running several marathons.

I hope you can see that this story has everything to do with order. It's easy to keep your day ordered when things go smoothly, but in the middle of crisis, it's even more important to create order. Likewise, keeping the "7 Fs" in order may be done peacefully, or may need to be done in the middle of chaos. In the end, it is always worth the work it takes.

Living an orderly life, and one that is balanced, is crucial. Our culture, like that of the cowboys, can be accidental or intentional. Recently, while attending a workshop about excellent business cultures, it was pointed out that we all have a "personal culture" in which we live. The culture is either unintentional, or it is intentional. An unintentional culture is one we live by default; and because of our selfish natures, it is a culture of self. Excellent cultures are intentional, and are exemplified by a life of service, rather than an attitude of self. Excellent cultures reveal an attitude of service. Cowboys, for the sake of community and survival, must live a more service-oriented life. That life is service-oriented—either toward people or animals—or it simply does not work. Livestock cannot live without care, and rural neighbors cannot get by without each other.

A great example is "branding time" at the ranches all across this country. This is an event whereby cowboys and cowgirls come from near and far to help with the branding of cattle for identification. There are many jobs at the branding corral. They include fire preparation and care, giving medications, and "marking" cattle with ear tags or brands. No one ever argues about which is the most important job. Everything gets done, by having common and shared goals. Food is prepared at midday or day-end, and the meal is a time of celebration. This is another example of intentional culture at its best.

Businesses with unhealthy cultures may have short-term success, but will never have long-term victories. Healthy cultures must be created intentionally and with great thought. In business, excellent cultures operate on true service and genuine care for team members. They examine motives of why they do what they do. They ask, "Are we giving our very best to workmates and customers alike?" They have clear and precise goals, and all team members agree that the goals are worthy and agreeable. They embrace real and candid communication. If knowing more about intentional business cultures appeals to you, then go to www.Excellent Cultures .com.

Finally, but most importantly, honoring your spiritual nature is very important. It is at the core of living in a healthy personal culture. An acquaintance of mine has been a very successful personal coach to a number of famous professional and collegiate athletes. As he starts to coach them, he always sees progress when they become more intentional about their chosen sports. He uses many techniques, like using track coaches for baseball players to help them be better "base stealers" and psychologists to help them get over negative thought patterns; and he personally coaches them on how to have a better culture of success. He's in his eighties now and will tell you that real breakthrough comes when each person he coaches goes back to their spiritual roots. He told me that when these athletes begin to honor God—by spending time with their Creator in a meaningful, intentional way—the breakthroughs become amazing.

How world-changing it would be if we all chose to intentionally spend quality time with our Creator, as the center feature of our personal culture.

CHAPTER 6

PUT NOTHING BEFORE GOD

We have hit on courage in all of our chapters so far. It takes courage to be humble before your Maker. It takes courage to live a life that honors others. It often takes courage to always be truthful and honest. It takes a great deal of bravery to keep your life in order, especially when you have to think of others, or in times of crisis. And in a world that is built around the "selfie," it takes courage to put God first in all things.

Let's go dig a little deeper in examining courage. We have heard "courage is defined by being afraid of something and then facing it anyway," or "being afraid to do something and doing it anyway." Cowboys, in the past and currently, face serious circumstances, some of which are even life-threatening. A rancher friend of mine rode his horse in his hundred-acre bull pasture with a sawed-off shotgun because the bulls were so aggressive and mean they would often try to charge and gore his horse. I arrived one day at his ranch and he had a bull in a "squeeze chute," with a shotgun slug hole in its right shoulder. You could reach into the hole and the bull did not even flinch. The bull had tried to take him out an hour before I arrived.

Many things, like mean cattle and stampedes, could take a cowboy's life. Weather, such as unseasonable snowstorms, could trap a cowboy in a life-threatening situation. Even accidents with equipment such as farm machinery can be a problem and at times be very dangerous. Branding cattle can cause injury from horseback, or as one works on the ground "doctoring" cattle. One friend was out riding a mountain trail one day when he and his horse slipped from a shale trail and fell several hundred feet down a steep embankment, rolling over and over. His dog went back to the ranch house several miles away. Seeing the dog alone, his wife realized he was in trouble.

Putting complete trust in God allows us to be more courageous. God expects us to use common sense. He also expects us, in my opinion, to plan and prepare well. But when faced with decisions which are not clear-cut, putting our trust in Him allows us to move ahead with great courage. It makes life a lot easier to know that He has our back.

Business decisions are not literally life threatening, but many decisions can be life changing for owners and employees alike. Layoffs, reprimands, and other financial decisions are sometimes very difficult to make. The results can have life-changing impacts on all concerned. Some businesspeople are apprehensive about doing things as important as employee reviews. Terminating employees is not anyone's favorite experience.

All of these things and many more are critical to owning, managing, or simply working in a company. In spite of the fact that these actions often produce great stress and tension, they must be done and must be done well. In spite of fear, one must be courageous to do these things in the most proactive and appropriate way.

Why is it that most people leave their mountains unclimbed, their potential unfulfilled, and the dreams turned into nightmares?

Philosophers, psychologists, and psychiatrists have made numerous studies and written thousands of books on this issue. But after all the layers have been stripped away, the answer is always the same: FEAR!

- We can't terminate an employee.
- We can't charge appropriate fees.
- We can't be in top-notch physical condition.
- We can't spend sufficient quality time with our spouse.

Call it what you want, but it's always some form of fear— fear that wasn't there from birth, but fear that was learned. As we see in the life of David in Scripture, God wants us to be courageous. At the same time we make difficult decisions, if we trust God for positive outcomes and turn to him for our direction, then we can move forward more fearlessly.

Maybe that's why the cowboy is courageous. From the time a cowboy is a small child, he, in everyday ranching life, has to face his fears and deal with them. Most cowboys I know are quite clear on Who is really in charge.

Let's get back to the story of my rancher friend. In the fall from the steep trail on horseback, his horse rolled over him several times, and he broke his pelvis and several ribs. His wife contacted neighboring ranchers and friends when his dog returned home alone, and they launched a search. It was early spring and the nights were very cold. Because of where he fell, he was not visible and was hidden back in a stand of timber. There was no obvious source of water nearby and he could not move. The search commenced and he was not found for two days. During that time, he dragged himself up to a boulder with a flat hollow surface and managed to drink dew that would accumulate during the night. He began to eat grasses which were close by. The pain would make him pass out periodically. And he told me he prayed a lot.

On the third day, a friend of mine found him by looking into that stand of trees. He was in "rough" shape. However, had he not been courageous, he would have died due to shock and panic. This is the way of the cowboy. The instinct is there for survival.

I would encourage you, the reader, to overcome fear that totally disables you on your quest for true freedom and inner peace. Things done intentionally in life are not easy, but the end results are always better.

CHAPTER 7

NO FOOLIN' AROUND WITH
ANOTHER FELLA'S GAL

All the things we discuss in this book lead to integrity. But in addressing it more directly, let's evaluate some more aspects.

A cowboy might say, "No foolin' around with another fella's gal." The cowboys I've known in my lifetime have high regard for family and other people's families. They are extremely polite, especially in front of women. In the cowboy culture, common expressions are "yes, ma'am" and "no, ma'am." I remember a story told by a cowboy friend of mine from a remote high desert ranch. He looks like a cowboy with his cowboy hat, "wild rag," vest, and packer boots because that's the way he dresses every day. On a cattle-buying trip in California, while eating lunch in a small restaurant, the waitress said to him in all sincerity, "I really like your cowboy costume." All he could say was "thank you, ma'am." I might have been dumbfounded enough that I don't know what I would have said.

There is nothing more deadly in a business than a boss messing around with female employees. When I first started in practice, I had a very wise and seasoned accountant tell me to never consider having an affair with an employee. He said nothing can kill a business faster than that. I have watched from a distance as marriages have been destroyed and businesses dismantled by illicit affairs.

Integrity is an interesting thing. It often has two sides for cowboys and in business. If we look at one of Aesop's famous fables, we can learn a very important business lesson based on the life of a farmer/rancher. A poor farmer, down on his luck and discouraged, one day notices a beautiful, glistening, golden egg next to his favorite goose. He, of course, feels that someone is playing a trick on him so he discards the egg in the trash. Then he starts to think about it and says "What the heck; what have I got to lose? I'll take the egg down to the assayer and find out what it's worth, if anything." Much to his surprise, he finds that it is solid gold! Of course, he is thrilled beyond his wildest dreams. The next day he comes back, and he finds another golden egg! Now, of course, he becomes very wealthy, to the point that he becomes very greedy and impatient. He wants those eggs now! So he devises this plan to kill the goose and get all her eggs. So, after he lops off her head and reaches inside he, of course, finds none.

I suggest that we can learn from that story about how to have a highly successful business. That business must be performed with high integrity, and that integrity must be lived out in their companies by understanding and then living with high values. Values are qualities that define us, our teams, and our organizations at their most basic level. They are the foundation on which expectations and trust (or distrust) are built. It's a critically important thing to establish clear and easily communicated values and then live them.

There are always two sides to success, the goose and the golden egg. Now what is the goose? The goose is the asset that produces the golden egg. The golden egg is what you want from the asset.

Now, if you adopt a pattern of business, which focuses only on what you want (the golden egg), and neglect the goose (liquidate the asset), you'll have no more of what you want—the golden eggs. Conversely, if you focus on the asset (the goose), with no aim toward the production you desire (the eggs), you won't have the wherewithal to feed the goose/asset. So you see, there must be balance.

Let's talk about the golden egg, or what we want from our profession. This list might include the following:

- Appreciation
- Recognition
- Achievement
- Compensation/benefits
- Open communication
- Responsibility/empowerment
- Advancement
- Profitability

If we focus on what we want without regard to the members of our business team, health of the business culture, vision, core values, and integrity, we undermine the very things that provide our fulfillment.

If we look at the goose/assets, what might they be in your business?

- The actual physical location
- The business model
- The business culture
- The humans

What's the most important asset? It's the human asset. The reason for that: It takes the human asset's input to determine how to use the other three. The humans can make a culture, which will determine the effectiveness of the other assets.

The farmer in the fable has one main failure: he lost his integrity.

Lust, pride, greed, and anger are the human emotions—especially for men—which lead to failure to act with integrity. In the cowboy's world, these emotions can be very dangerous, to the point of leading to personal injury or even death. But of course, this is not unique to only cowboys. Each of us will have to make many decisions in our lives based on our personal integrity. In the end, a life well lived is a life lived with the highest measure of integrity. The only "value system" I know of which establishes the nature of integrity is God's.

CHAPTER 8

DON'T KILL THE DREAMS
OF OTHERS

Words can either create life or they can kill. Understanding this one principle would have a very positive impact on the world.

"Home on the Range" is a familiar song written in 1876 by Dr. Brewster Higley. John Lomax rewrote the lyrics of the chorus in 1910. Here are some of the words:

> Home, home on the range,
> Where the deer and the antelope play,
> Where seldom is heard a discouraging word
> And the skies are not cloudy all day.

The third line is interesting. "Where seldom is heard a discouraging word" rings with the positive outlook of people of the middle to late 1800s who were in the process of seeking new adventures and opportunities in the West. Being negative was not only counterintuitive to them, but was also very counterproductive.

In the cowboy's world, his words of encouragement are for people and animals. Kind, quiet, gentle words work far better with anxious horses, as well as many other animals. They also work better with people. Being firm in our speech when necessary can also be done with a caring but firm attitude. Cowboys and businessmen need to guide, and at times help, others change their behavior. I have seen many a cowboy, with a firm voice and direct eye contact, correct a young buckaroo in the branding pen or when handling cattle as they are moved to different pastures. But a cowboy is also known for saying very few words. I believe the less we speak and the more we listen, the better off everybody is. And the more we encourage and the less we criticize, the better are the people we lead.

In my coaching practice, I've found this to be especially true. Asking "big" questions and letting the other person find their own answers is often much more productive than telling them what to do.

As an executive coach, I have found that asking powerful questions works the very best in helping people achieve personal excellence. As people make change, they must be the initiators of that change. You cannot tell a person what to do and expect them to truly "buy in." The responsibility of a coach is largely to help other people achieve their dreams and fulfill their God-given purpose.

How do cowboys teach their children on a ranch with all the ranching responsibilities? Quite surprisingly, their children learn by osmosis. What do I mean by that?

When my oldest granddaughter was five, I taught her to drive my flatbed truck in low gear, low four-wheel drive, across a pasture, while I fed cows with hay bales out of the back of the truck. Her feet, of course, could not reach the pedals. After feeding, I would have to jump back into the cab of the moving truck to stop it. I used a few firm words to tell her what to do. She was frightened at first, but with a few words of encouragement she was a pro. How do you think she felt when she returned to her home on the ranch and told her mom and dad what she was able to accomplish? On the ranch, my grandchildren drive ATVs, trucks, and tractors long before they are old enough to have driver's licenses.

Two rancher friends of mine, when they were age six (they are cousins), drove a hay truck during haying season. Because the truck had a stick shift, one got down on the floor and pushed the clutch and brake pedals, while the other gave directions and steered the truck, standing on the driver's seat. Obviously, they had to take turns or there would have been "hell to pay." Imagine the words spoken in that situation.

Isn't business a lot like the experience of those two six-year-olds? Neither one of them could have driven that truck alone. When we work as a team, we often have distinct roles in reaching our goals. Sometimes we can't see what another person sees—yet—and we move ahead in faith. It's this accumulation of individual effort of people working together which multiplies what all the team members can accomplish individually. When we work with others, giving them positive encouragement is much more powerful than exercising the "gift of the critical spirit." In the end, for our business to be successful, we must nurture each other's dreams and celebrate each other's victories.

A rancher friend of mine in eastern Oregon was driving home from town one day when he spotted a herd of deer running across a steep hillside. They were obviously frightened. As he looked up the hill behind them, he saw a pack of coyotes chasing them from behind. Amazingly, he realized they were actually being herded toward a cliff out a distance in front of his truck. Lo and behold, as the chase unfolded, several of the deer, too exhausted to change direction, actually ran off the cliff to their deaths. Clever, those coyotes. My friend watched in amazement as the coyotes skirted the cliff and came down to where the deer had fallen and began to drag them off away from the road. Now that's killing someone else's dreams for sure.

In business, it's not unusual for leaders to drive employees to their own professional deaths. Leadership is such a huge responsibility and should never be taken lightly. It's critical as leaders to not kill other people's dreams.

Finally, the sport of rodeo grew out of the cowboy's time off from traditional work chores. There were bets and challenges to each other to see if they could "ride the bronc" or rope that steer in the fastest time or in the best style. Cowboys to this day in the sport of rodeo are great encouragers, even of their competition. What a great lesson we could take to our business. I always maintained in my business that we were never in competition with other businesses. We were in competition for people's spendable dollars. That's a big philosophical difference.

CHAPTER 9

WATCH YOUR MOUTH

Only a few times have I seen a cowboy "go off" verbally. Cowboys are known for their "quiet strength." Listening and paying attention to everything around them is their normal behavior. It has to be. They will carefully evaluate every animal in the herd, checking their behavior and their health. As they ride horseback, they are always checking fencing or evaluating how much feed remains in a pasture. They are constantly on the lookout for dangers to their livestock in downed barbed wire, mineral block shortages, and predators. *Watching* and *listening* is what makes them successful. As managers of land and animals, they must pay attention to every detail.

Saying nothing is often the best form of communication. Saint Francis of Assisi has been credited with the saying "Spread the good news; if all else fails, use words." The cowboy way of putting this might be "Damn what they say. Watch what they do, and you'll know who they are."

Cowboys frequently lead by example and not by words. On the bank of the Colorado River in Texas a young "cow puncher" was asked to take the lead in swimming the herd across. He said that while he was not a good swimmer and was afraid of the water, "I am a hired hand and will not shirk my duty." By the way, as the story is told, he made it across. He truly led by example, and did not give a lecture on bravery. He showed what he was made of by example.

The image of the cowboy seems to be a great example of this principle. Be tough, remain quiet, and lead by example. Look at old western movies and you will see this in action.

One winter our Australian shepherd stock dog thought there was work to do across a frozen pond. Unfortunately the ice was thin, and halfway across she went through into the water. Each move she made to get back up on the ice only broke small pieces away, and she was getting exhausted. Fortunately, my wife noticed what happened and came to get me. We both knew that if we tried to go out on the ice, we would go through and probably drown. We kept encouraging the dog and tried to talk her into persevering. However, she was losing the battle. The encouragement of our words was just not enough. I ran to the barn and grabbed a lariat, and when I got back to the pond, she was just about to give up all hope. I threw a loop out over her, and even though she was a long way off I was able to get the loop around her neck. With some careful pulling we got her back to shore and into the house, to help her recover from her hypothermia.

Saying encouraging words are vital but sometimes they are too little, too late. That's why I recommend that leaders constantly give positive affirmation to their team. I too have fallen into the trap of too much correction and not enough affirmation and lost team members over it.

Sometimes we read something that sticks with us forever. I remember reading Lee Iacocca's biography, in which one thing really stood out for me. That one thing was, as he took over at Chrysler and turned the business around, he made a habit of going into the factory and walking up to people on the assembly line, asking how they were doing and letting them know he cared—by the positive words out of his mouth. People in every area of business love to have positive words of affirmation. A negative word never motivates anyone. If positive affirmation is used in your business, with a true spirit of caring, it would be one of the ingredients for massive success. It doesn't take a lot of words to show people you care about them. Celebrations of small successes, a few kind words, being interested in team members' families, and showing respect for others go a long way to having people buy in. When they feel honored and respected, they become committed to your vision and are willing to crawl over broken glass to accomplish those goals.

"Watching your mouth" can also refer to self-talk. People often talk about being true to one's self. People interpret this to mean that when one doesn't like something—even something to which one has committed oneself—then the proper thing to do is to quit. There is no quit in a cowboy.

On one particular occasion, I was riding to gather fall cattle in a snowstorm. The trail boss knew the country well, but several of us did not. He decided to do a sweep on horseback of a mountainous allotment, and decided to drop one cowboy off to watch a "draw" the cattle might move through. The trail boss told this cowboy to stay exactly where he dismounted and wait there. Our sweep took several hours, and when we returned to the place where the first cowboy was situated, we almost couldn't find him. There he stood, just as we had left him, covered in snow, which had been falling heavily. It made him nearly invisible. An absolute rule we have always followed when we are on a large ranch or in the wilderness is that if you become lost, do not move. If you stay put, the others will find you. If you start wandering around, it makes it very hard for rescuers to figure out where you are. In this case, needless to say, we had to build a fire to thaw him out. If he had moved from his position, with the amount of snow that had fallen, we might not have found him.

Inappropriate words can be manifested in business in a huge way. The rub comes in when people *feel* they are committed, instead of *being* committed. As time passes, obstacles are encountered. The obstacles may be as simple as our decision-maker being alone in his or her environment with no accountability. Or a person might have a wonderful project, only to have others discount it. These circumstances can precipitate negative actions and words. Now alone and discouraged, a process of speech begins which has these predictable steps:

Rationalization turns to *manipulation*, which in turn leads to *perpetration* (devaluing other people) and causes *defamation*. The end result is that the person we are discussing begins a process of lying to cover up for the lack of his or her own personal value.

This sounds complicated, but it all starts with our person not understanding the difference between *being* committed and *feeling* committed. Feeling committed is a function of the limbic system of one's mind. Our limbic system can be very deceiving. Being committed starts in our cerebral cortex and involves words that connect with our inner spirit and will help us be committed to our perceived purpose. These are called "positive affirmations." *Feeling* committed is short-term; *being* committed is for life. That's why New Year's resolutions never stick.

This whole discussion of self-talk can highlight the differences between a cowboy and our person who only feels committed. Just feeling committed, for a cowboy, can be very dangerous and can lead to personal injury or death. We saw that with our snow-covered cowboy. Maybe it's because a cowboy must at times be self-reliant, and at other times he must completely rely on others. Feeling committed instead of being committed can be lethal in any organization.

An example of this in everyday cowboy life can be highlighted by an experience I had elk hunting in Wyoming. We were hunting at very high altitude, and one of the young men in camp was a "tenderfoot dude" from the East Coast. The night before the opening of the season, while sitting in camp twenty miles from the nearest trailhead, I watched as this young man decided to display his masculinity by drinking himself into a stupor. The rest of us were *committed* to a serious hunt, in the presence of many grizzly bears. We knew these bears had moved into the area in large number due to fires in Yellowstone that year.

The next day this young man and his father went on to a higher altitude, above 7000 feet, with a guide to hunt in another area. In the middle of the night, the guide came racing back into our camp on horseback to say that he thought the young man was dying. He then continued on to the trailhead twenty miles away and drove into Cody to get help from first responders.

In the morning, when the light of day was sufficient, the first responders were able to reach this young man and his father by helicopter. The father was terrified and the young man was delirious. They were able to get him down to Cody and to the hospital. He was diagnosed with alcohol-related altitude sickness. Fortunately, at the lower elevation he quickly recovered. During that night, his life hung in the balance. He was a very lucky young man. The circumstances were from *feeling* committed to the hunt and not actually taking in all the risks and possibilities. He was, as a result, not physically prepared.

The night before, we had to watch our mouths, because he was clearly not open to correction. This was probably a case where words of correction before the fact would not have been valuable. Living life out of his feelings almost proved to be fatal for him.

CHAPTER 10

DON'T TAKE WHAT AIN'T YOURS

In the old West, and as is true today, some of the fine points of cowboy code dictate horseman etiquette. No one borrowed a horse from another man's string without his permission. That permission was rarely given. One never abuses someone else's horse.

The practicality of not taking another man's horse can be illustrated by a situation I was part of a few years ago. On a day of miserable weather, after a morning deer hunt, we had all stopped to gather up and visit. Someone shot a deer that morning, and a cowboy friend's son went to gather the deer and bring it back down to the trucks. He jumped on an unfamiliar horse and rode off. The next thing we knew, while we stood visiting, the horse came running back to our gathering, missing its rider. It turns out that our young cowboy had located the deer and threw a rope around its horns. As he began to drag it out into the open, the horns hooked on some sage and spooked the horse he was riding. Clearly he did not know the intricate behavior of that particular horse. The horse bucked him off and he was knocked unconscious. Some of the cowboys went looking for him, while I jumped on my horse to get a truck to take him to John Day Hospital, thirty-five miles away. By the time we got him loaded in the truck he had regained consciousness, and when we got him to the hospital he checked out just fine in the emergency room. The only thing really injured was his ego. Taking a horse he was not totally familiar with might have been very costly, however.

In business, things can get really magnified when taking what's not yours. Often things will snowball from small indiscretions to larger issues. Years ago I taught my team to be careful about what they take. For instance, it's not uncommon for employees to use office postage for personal mail and think nothing of it. Even the boss will sometimes feel justified in that practice. Unfortunately, those things can escalate. Many businesses have zero tolerance for taking what's not yours. A friend of mine borrowed someone else's bicycle from work on the weekend, with every intention of returning it after using it. Sadly enough, the bicycle belonged to a manager who came in to work on a project that weekend and discovered it missing. This friend of mine did not have intentions of stealing the bike, but was terminated from his job anyway.

In life, it is not a stretch to say that small indiscretions often lead to bigger ones, until our entire integrity will eventually be called into question. We don't have to look any further than Wall Street to see this lived out in an outrageous way. In government and news media we see this played out over and over again. As a result, we have lower trust for our leaders than at almost any time in history.

In the cowboy culture, as it relates to ranching, there are definite ways to identify owners of livestock. Horses and cows are branded with firebrands or freeze brands. Of course, we have heard of cattle-rustling, and it is often a theme in old western movies. Cattle-rustling is still a problem to this day. In my life experience, however, I have been witness to nothing but honesty.

Fences are also a way of identifying ownership. It's not unusual for cattle to get through fences to neighboring ranches, and the common courtesy is to let the owner know you have their cows. I personally have fed and cared for the cattle of a neighboring rancher for days to weeks until the owner could come and retrieve his livestock. In a ranching community, it is imperative that you honor each other with high integrity; otherwise, the community relationships and support will fall apart. Ranching communities rely on neighbors and friends for survival.

Wouldn't it be nice if we had the same frame of mind in our own businesses? You see, we are in the same organization, and if we have a healthy business culture and common goals, we wouldn't think of taking advantage of each other. Do some people have major character flaws, which hinder their integrity? I personally believe this is somewhat rare, and is pathology uncommon to most organizations. Of course, there are those who are not able to act with integrity due to these dysfunctional traits. Let us focus on what is more normal, and that is that most teams can focus on common values and purpose so that team members want to strive for those common goals.

Another area of taking what's not yours can raise its ugly head in business competition. People become so obsessed with competing with other businesses that they compromise their integrity in so doing. It may be naïve, but my philosophy has always been that we are not in competition with each other; we are in competition for the consumers' "spendable dollars." As we focus on this principle, we can spend our energy to identify what people need, and then meet that need. This is a win-win and can feel so much more rewarding when we accomplish our goals.

CHAPTER 11

DON'T BE HANKERING FOR YOUR BUDDY'S STUFF

A story from Luke 16:14–16 is very interesting:

> Now the Pharisees, who were lovers of money, also heard all these things, and they derided [Jesus]. And He said to them. "You are those who justify yourselves before men, but God knows your hearts. For what is highly esteemed among men is an abomination in the sight of God. The law and the prophets were until John. Since that time the kingdom of God has been preached, and everyone is pressing into it."

This occurs in the middle of a chapter about money. Now we're "talking turkey" when it comes to business. Isn't it all about money? Or, maybe not. It's amazing that Jesus said more about money than any other topic. One-sixth of the Gospels of Matthew, Mark, and Luke talk about money. Twelve of the thirty-eight parables Jesus used in teaching are about money. A recent study suggests that an average adult American male spends fifty percent of his time dealing with money-related matters.

Let's go ahead with our story. This appears in the middle of a chapter that is almost entirely focused on money. The real story here is about covetousness. The Pharisees taught that the godlier one was, the more money he had. They were the original "prosperity gospel" preachers. They set all their values on wealth, and not on love, truth, or grace.

Where do you place money in your life? Where do you place money in your business? Is it the only goal? Those with money seem to be highly esteemed in our modern society, but when we go to heaven we will be in for some big surprises. "The least shall be first and the first shall be last" (that's my paraphrase).

Solomon reflected on his life after falling into carnality in the book of Ecclesiastes: "there is nothing new under the sun" (Eccl. 1:9). His conclusions were that all the good things he had received—great wisdom, great wealth, and more of everything than anyone has had before or since—meant nothing when out of the context of being reverent of God and valuing real relationships. When we are dead and gone, people will not remember us for our possessions but rather for the "stories" we created as we were more concerned with other people's needs. You can take that to the bank.

Although cowboys are seen somewhat as rugged individualists, they know the value of great relationships. They are most likely to enjoy the company of others and know the meaning of working together for a common purpose. They really know the meaning of the saying "If you want to have a friend, then be a friend." Their lives and livelihood depend on it.

If we analyze others by what they have, what they wear, what they drive, or how big their house is, it will lead to real and regular covetousness. In other words, it will lead to simply wanting more of what one already has. That's the definition of covetousness. (The next section of Luke 16 tells another connected story. It's about a rich man and Lazarus. It's readily available for you to read and I'll let you do that on your own. Trust me, it's worth reading and really meditating on.)

It's interesting to note that a truly healthy business culture's number one characteristic is a "culture of service." There's a huge irony here: When we focus on money as our number one objective, we miss many real opportunities. When we focus on service, not only is our career more rewarding but the benefits come along naturally. It not only fits with God's economy but it works as He intended it to.

There's another interesting point to be mentioned. The Bible gives us a promise which "we can hang our hat on." In Malachi 3:10, God says:

> "Bring all the tithes into the storehouse
> That there may be food in My house,
> And try Me in this,"
> Says the LORD of hosts.
> "If I will not open for you the windows of heaven
> And pour out for you such blessing
> That there will not be room enough to receive it."

How very interesting. Not only does covetousness eat us up, but in dramatic contrast, giving away what we have as a priority is rewarded beyond our wildest dreams. It's a guarantee. God even says, "try Me in this."

How does our cowboy look at all of this? Those I know are thankful for hard work; appreciate and take great care of what they have; are glad their "office" is open to the sky (even when some days deliver serious weather-related difficulties); and value honesty, friends, family, and God. They might admire another man's horse or his saddle, but they are not covetous about others' possessions. Some own ranches and some do day work. Some try to grow their agricultural businesses and some are satisfied to "work for the brand." Most cowboys I know have solid values and principles that guide their lives. They know that their friends and coworkers are important. They give their all every day, in life in the saddle or out of it. They also know how to stop now and then to laugh and have some fun. And their "word" is their bond. If more businesses followed the cowboy way, the world would be a better place. And you can take that to the bank, too.

CHAPTER 12

A LOOK AT THE VALUE OF THESE 10 COMMANDMENTS

Why should anyone even aspire to the fulfillment of the Ten Commandments in their life? The Ten Commandments are a "tutor." They help to point us to good character. Why is your character so important? Who are we as humans? God created us to be of good character, so that He could use us for His purposes.

I was recently watching a TV program which highlighted the work of the Jalen Rose Foundation. Jalen Rose was a member of the University of Michigan "Fab Five" and played for a national championship with his teammates. He played for thirteen years in the NBA and played for a world championship while with the Indiana Pacers. After his retirement, he established a foundation. One of the foundation's goals was to help educate inner-city young people in Detroit. Although he was a famous basketball player, his fame as an athlete does not measure up to the true purpose for his life. His real life's purpose is to help these inner-city kids become successful. To do this he established the Jalen Rose Academy through his foundation. It has open enrollment, and they have invited young people from all over Detroit to attend. The students are kids who really had no hope for successful futures.

When he was interviewed about the progress of these students, he explained that the school's focus was on academics, leadership, and, most of all, on developing good character. He went on to explain how one's character must be intact, so that that these young people can be good citizens and contributors to society in a positive way. If one does not feel good about their character, they cannot be positive citizens. It just seems so obvious that one's character, more than any other factor, determines one's success.

What is character? One dictionary definition is "the mental and moral qualities distinctive to an individual." It includes the personality, nature, disposition, temperament, temper, mentality, makeup, and much more. So the question we might ask is this: How do the commandments we have discussed manifest themselves in people to create good character?

Truth, honesty, being your word, following through on what you say, and eye-to-eye contact during communication are all pieces of good character. God tells us about good character traits as "the fruit of the Spirit." Galatians 5:22–23 says these traits are love, joy, peace, longsuffering, kindness, goodness, faithfulness, gentleness, and self-control. The author concludes, "Against these things there is no law."

A smile is a great example. A smile demonstrates all of these great characteristics. As I practiced orthodontics, I frequently talked about the value of a smile. My associate gave me this quote:

> A smile costs nothing, but gives so much. It enriches those who receive, without making poorer those who give. It takes but a moment, but the memory of it sometimes lasts forever.
>
> None is so rich or mighty that he can get along without it, and none is so poor but that he can be made rich with it. A smile creates happiness in the home, fosters good will in business, and is the countersign of friendship.
>
> It brings rest to the weary, cheer to the discouraged, sunshine to the sad, and it is nature's best antidote for trouble. Yet it cannot be bought, begged, borrowed, or stolen, for it is sometimes of no value to anyone until it is given away.
>
> Some people are too tired to give a smile. Give them one of yours, as none needs a smile so much as he who has no more to give.

We used this as a philosophy of practice and lived by this tenet. It is a simple manifestation of one of the qualities of character.

I personally have never known a cowboy with a mean-spirited attitude. Most I know are quick with a warm smile and positive attitude. I think this helps them deal with very tough lives and the problems that come at them daily. Many of them do not make a lot of money but they are honest, hardworking people of good character. By contrast, look at the problems of the inner city, where families have a history of living on welfare. Many of these people have lost more than work ethic and strong values. They have lost their character. This is a tragedy.

It takes good character for people to be attracted to you. Why are they attracted to you? It is because they like you and *trust* you. It's why Jalen Rose knows that for long-term success, one must first be of good character.

As Ken Blanchard points out in his book *Raving Fans*, it is with good character that we are able to make deposits in the "emotional bank accounts" of people around us. This is especially true in the lives of people who must trust us to be in relationship with us. Our commitment to our character and to integrity, our genuine interest in others, our enthusiasm, and exceeding others' expectations contributes greatly to long-lasting relationships. Long-lasting relationships contribute ultimately to business success.

Your character also contributes to your commitment to excellence in any chosen endeavor. The world is crying for people who care. One old adage is "People don't care how much you know, until they know how much you care." Our character and integrity will not hide our commitment to excellence—they will declare it. Excellence is an attitude.

Good character also manifests itself when we are confronted with change, or with a need to change. If we always start with the focus on character as the underpinning to our answers to life's problems, then we'll know when a change must be made. It's my experience in ranching that when your character is intact, you make better decisions for your animals and for the people around you as well.

All advances in humankind were because someone was willing to change, to see things differently. If we are living by the commandments to the best of our ability (thank God we live under His amazing grace), we will be much more willing to make changes when needed.

There are really only two kinds of change. There is actual change, physical change. Examples would be when we have to change a tire, or in business when we have to change our prices or fees. We might have to terminate an employee, or we might have to start attending church.

There is also psychological change. The manifestation of that might be when we have to change our minds, or when we have to accept something that in the past we found unacceptable. This is frequently experienced in regard to our faith. If we have struggled in our relationship with God, perhaps we might find ourselves in a position of accepting His immense love or forgiveness. When we make this kind of change in our beliefs, things will get better immediately.

Fear gets in the way of many people finding what adds meaning to their lives. Possibilities are closed off. Who said change should be feared? Isn't it great to be around people of good character who are not afraid of change? We might call these people "fearless."

Cowboys face change every day. They experience change in weather, animal health, fence conditions, and many other variables that make a routine day nearly impossible. But their foundation in good character makes them able to deal with change. Change is exciting. It can be the staff of life. If we were not able to change, how would we ever become all that God desires of us? A willingness or desire to change is the missing ingredient in so many lives. The supposed risk is small when compared to the potential gain.

In the cowboy's life there are a series of decisions wrapped around things that must, by necessity, be changed and changed quickly. Frequently he must make changes at a moment's notice. These changes often have life-or-death significance. Business is no different. Many changes may be of life-or-death importance (for the business) as well. Railroads are a classic example of resistance to change. If they had seen themselves as transportation and shipping businesses, instead of just railroads, they might now have the airlines, buses, and all transportation businesses working under their umbrella. Change is necessary to keep moving in a positive direction. I am sure you will, as the reader, think of many more examples.

When there is doubt about a particular situation, focus on it intensely and bring it to God, and then keep on going the way you are going. Only make a change when there is no doubt the change will be for the better. In actual practice, to build your character, consider a "change a week" program and see where God takes you.

CHAPTER 13

LEADERSHIP

Another part of great character is the ability to be a great leader when called upon. Leadership is shaped by the commandments we have discussed. Proverbs 29:18 (KJV) says, "Where there is no vision, the people perish." Leaders, whether they are cowboys or businessmen, are the "keepers of the vision" in their perspective worlds. And a vision cannot be created without good character. And good leaders, whether cowboys or businessmen, must intuitively know what it takes to be great leaders.

God "purposes" leaders to lead. They must have clarity of the vision. They must know exactly what they are being called to. The vision must be ethical. The leader must be committed to the vision. Eventually, the people they lead must be committed to the vision. There must be a precise game plan to achieve the result. And there must be constant repetition of the principles for success.

Of course, the leader must be leading from out front. They are, after all, ultimately responsible under God's authority for the success of their operation, whether it is business, a ranch, or even their family. They make the hard decisions, and they must have the courage to do whatever it takes to get the job done.

With great character, one can live with a "fearless heart." It's exciting to hear people outline their vision with its great potential—the first step of your journey to fulfill your dreams. People start out excited to make a difference on the planet, to be all they can be, to dream the dream. But why is it that for most people the mountain is left unclimbed, the potential unfulfilled, and the dream turned into a nightmare?

Fear wasn't present when we were born. We were God-created and perfect in His eyes at birth. As we live our lives, fear is learned. And the older we get, sometimes the more handicapped we become. This fear we acquire sometimes totally disables us on our quest for true freedom and inner peace.

History indicates that the most successful combatants against fear were people who were unconditionally committed to a noble cause. Like the early Christians, and even the courageous Christian martyrs of long ago and today, these people knew that in order to truly live, they had to accept their own deaths. Of course, Christ set the ultimate example.

Recently I saw a poster of a cowboy on a bucking horse. He was having a wild ride. The caption on the poster said, "True success is overcoming the fear of being successful." Unfortunately, in life and in business, the "baddest" people one faces are themselves. Apparently, the poster was the picture of a young lady's dad. Under the picture she wrote; "My

Dad—He rode broncos for many years and coached count- less kids chasing their dreams. I can hear him in my head hollering 'Gas it, lift, charge.' And that's life, folks. If you are serious—I mean dead serious—about reaching your goals and being successful you have to 'gas it.' Get in time, let loose of those swells, and go for it! Lift on your reins and charge!" After all, life is an adventure and nothing can be gained by holding back and being afraid.

In looking at our own character, it can be said that the spiritual aspect of valor is evidenced by composure—a calm peace of mind. Tranquility is courage in repose. Truly brave people are ever serene; they are never taken by surprise; noth- ing ruffles the equanimity of their spirit. In the heart of the battle they remain cool; in the midst of catastrophes they keep level minds. Earthquakes do not shake them; they laugh at storms. We admire those as truly great who, in the menac- ing presence of danger or death, retain their composure.

Cowboys I have known exemplify this attitude of com- posure. For example, a raging bull can be something to be reckoned with. You'll remember my story of my cowboy friend who had a bull in their bull pasture attack him and his horse while he was "riding herd." If it had not been for his quick thinking and his preparation, his experience might have been fatal. As the "red-eyed" bull charged, he pulled a weapon and shot the bull in the front shoulder. In order to explain how tough an 1,800-pound bull can be, the shot he fired only distracted the bull long enough to allow him to ride at full speed out of the pasture. The bull, of course, recovered completely.

Three anecdotal stories I lived out are horse stories that show courage is "bucking up" even when you don't feel like it. The first story involves a rope horse I owned that could not stand to have a rope touch his front legs. That's a big problem if you don't catch every steer you throw a rope at. When you try to catch a steer by the horns and you miss, the rope often comes back and hits your horse in the front legs. When the rope hit his front legs, he would launch into a "bucking fit." I tried every technique I knew of and that had been suggested by good horse trainers; I could never resolve the problem.

One night at a practice, roping after missing a steer, the rope came back and began what was to be an experience the cowboy never looks forward to. As my horse began to launch into one of his "fits," I lost a stirrup; the next thing I knew I was what seemed like twenty feet in the air. Later several of the other ropers said that they had never seen a cowboy fly so high. I hit the ground flat on my back, and after regaining my composure (and air to breathe), I collected my hat and my horse.

The lesson here is that would have been very easy to quit roping that night, load my horse in the trailer, and head home. However, as every cowboy knows, you don't have a choice. You have to get back on and continue to ride. Is it because you have to look tough? No. It's because if the horse knows he can get you on the ground, he will do everything in his power to make it happen again.

Business and life are very similar. We often need to "climb back in the saddle," make some corrections, and then go for it again. That is all part of leadership. (By the way, I ended up selling the horse. Flying through the air was not my favorite activity.)

The second story had more dire consequences. I was roping cattle by myself one fine afternoon (message: never rope alone), and after catching a "lead steer" I stopped and began to back my horse up slightly. What I did not know was that the horse's bit had broken inside his mouth. The sharp end poked him in the roof of the mouth and because he was a superb athlete, he jumped and "sun-fished" over backwards. I knew I was in trouble and could see him planting the saddle horn in the middle of my chest. As a result, I dove over to the side and landed on my shoulder and my neck. I could hear the bones breaking, and for a few minutes I lay there checking to make sure I had not broken my neck. After getting my breath, and doing my medical evaluation, I knew I could move my legs. Things were still not good and so I crawled over to where my son was working and told him to take me to the hospital. After further evaluation the doctor told me I had broken my collarbone in several places (later requiring surgery) and fractured three ribs.

Why do I tell this story? In the middle of crisis, leaders need to make wise decisions and do what it takes to keep the ship afloat. There are times when leaders feel lonely and under attack, but they must persevere. Staying mentally fit to make tough decisions in difficult circumstances can save a cowboy's life, or can save a businessman's career.

The third story involves a different set of circumstances. One day while team roping, I was chasing a steer roped by another cowboy. My goal was to catch the steer by his hind legs. My heel horse at the time was very solid and experienced, but I committed a "driver's error." As I came around the corner to swing my rope in front of the steer's hind legs, I cut the corner and leaned too far off the left side of my horse, causing him to actually fall over on his left side while running at a gallop. As you can imagine, he landed on my left leg full force. In this case, the good news was that I keep our arena ground soft by grooming it regularly and I was not injured but only bruised.

The moral to this story is that leaders must not only have a plan, but must execute the plan with great vision and skill. Not doing each part of your job accurately and efficiently can sometimes lead to disaster. In business, the leader must have a great and crystal-clear vision; he must teach those around him so that the vision is clear, and he must lead his team with wisdom and fearlessness.

Hopefully, you can see that one's character is critical to surviving and thriving in our lives. Leading must be done intentionally, and the leader must be fearless. These characteristics are so often lacking. These stories I've mixed in highlight the need to behave in ways that are pleasing to God. Attempting to follow His commandments will categorically change your life and allow you be all that God intended you to be. Take on the adventure.

CHAPTER 14

BACK TO THE EARTH

A part of the cowboy life often involves farming. We have one thirty-acre hay field at the north end of our ranch and due to the condition of the field, this was the year to rework it. I can summarize much of what we've learned on this journey by letting you follow me through that process.

This fall we started the removing the old crop because its usefulness was diminished and productive quality had diminished. Why had it become less productive? You only had to drive a tractor across it to see the answer. If one wore dentures, they would have lost them during that tractor ride. The attack of the "alien varmints" made it so rough that I was concerned for the wear and tear on equipment such as our tractors, baler, and rake. There are several reasons. First of all, this field had alfalfa and orchard grass. These plants have a useful life span, and the age and life span of these plants made the field less fruitful. Some of you might relate to this. In business, we see cycles as well. Sometimes our businesses are very productive, and other times they seem to stall out.

In addition, the field was exceptionally infested with rodents. We had pocket gophers, voles, and ground squirrels taking over every area of the field. In business, there are "predators" who invade, and they can kill and destroy the business. What are these predators? They can be lack of vision, laziness, unhealthy culture, inappropriate goals, and lack of action steps, as well as unqualified employees and poor leaders. Nothing in farming and nothing in business is static.

So what do we do? In the fall, we used a disc to cut the sod in the field into small pieces. Then I used a rollover plow to turn the sod over, so that the plant material was essentially buried. Any of this sound familiar in a business setting? In business, it is often appropriate to dissect the problems into small, manageable sections. After making the pieces more manageable, we can then roll over the things that are not working and eliminate them.

I then left the field in this state all winter for the plant material to decompose. The varmints lost their homes, and the field became more manageable for the spring.

Isn't that just like making course corrections in business? We identify the problems and make them more manageable. We try to identify the "rodents" and eliminate them. Then we take time to let the efforts we've made settle in, and observe if our efforts were effective.

In the spring, we continued to disc the field some more to break up the soil and prepare it for planting. Not all the varmints were gone, and the problematic sod had to be broken up some more to create a good seed bed. Just like in business, we have to take steps to build a good "seed bed" or "culture," to have greater success so that the seeds (our ideas) will grow.

We continued to eliminate the varmints and level the field so that we could drive over it without ruining equipment on rough terrain during the harvest. We had to prepare the field to have a level seed bed. Just as in business, we have to continue to remove the growth-restricting obstacles and level the playing field, so that there are less bumps for the team and to create greater success. The key is that our field was producing, but it was not as productive at it should have been. Does that sound familiar to any businesspeople reading this?

Finally, we planted the seed. The seed, however, is an annual seed that will be harvested mid-season, and then the "discing" and planting process will be done all over again. The rotation crop allows plant toxins from the previous crop to dissipate, making the soil healthier. It also tends to naturally eliminate more of the weeds. In business, we see the same principles apply. We need to be ever vigilant to continue to eliminate the weeds, toxins, and problem areas, so that the business will thrive.

After the rotation crop is harvested and the new perennial seed is planted, we are ready for a series of seasons, weather permitting, of bountiful harvest. Exactly like business, there are cycles. Great attention is necessary to keep problem areas from controlling the culture and the fruitful growth of the business.

Incidentally, the seed which we planted was dead for all practical purposes until we prepared a good seed bed, provided water and fertilizer, and kept the weeds and varmints out of the mix. After careful farming and these amendments, the seed came to life.

Many people and businesses are just like that. For all practical purposes they are "dead." These same principles must be applied to bring them back to life. They need proper leadership, vision, and motivation to be raised to life from death. Unfortunately, many businesses do not pay attention to detail and function intentionally. As a result, they either fail or limp along aimlessly.

In my experience, effective coaching can make all the difference in the world in helping people and businesses perform at peak levels and soar to the top. Cowboys who farm, and farmers who farm, understand this all too well. A couple of crop failures tend to be great "teachers" in agriculture and in other businesses.

All of the principles we have discussed play a role in avoiding "crop failures." When we live intentionally, understand how to create healthy visions and healthy cultures, and accomplish these with appropriate "action steps," we have greater chances for success.

In farming, there are variables which can't be avoided. There are weather and harsh environmental conditions. There are also completely unanticipated circumstances. But a good farm plan with excellent execution and attention to detail gives us the best shot at success. Good soil and good seed are more likely to germinate. If I were to just broadcast the seed over a field of weeds, the chances of success would be zero. In business, action without vision, a plan, action steps, and unconditional commitment will usually meet with failure. A business without an intentional culture will surely "starve out."

Now we can see that doing things the cowboy way usually gives a better chance for success in all areas of life. Actually, doing things God's way will be fruitful, in His economy and according to His plan every time. He is the Master of bringing life from death.

CHAPTER 15

LESSONS FROM TEAM ROPING

One of my avocations is team roping. It's an old event which grew out of the cowboy's desire to have a recreational pastime at the end of a long working week. Cowboys, by necessity, had to catch cattle to "doctor" them or "brand" them for identification and clarify ownership. Occasionally they had to catch a mamma cow that was struggling to help deliver her calf. During times of relaxation cowboys devised ways to compete with each other to see who could be the best at roping cattle. Many of the modern-day rodeo events grew out of this recreation and competition between working cowboys.

Team roping brings together five "beating hearts" to accomplish a coordinated goal. There are two cowboys, two horses, and a horned cow (usually Corrientes, a Mexican breed of horned cows). The cowboys start on either side of a chute in what is called the "box." One is for the "header" (who catches the cow by the horns), and one is for the "heeler" (who catches the cow by the hind legs). The steer is released from the chute. The two cowboys, two horses, and steer have to all come together in perfect synchronization to complete the event. This is a timed event, which means the fastest team wins. At the time of this writing, the world record was set at a National Finals Rodeo and is 3.3 seconds.

When I teach on team building, I use the team roping as an example of how coordinated business teams must be for incredible efficiency. Each cowboy (leader) plays a very key role. Each horse (team member) must be trained and then guided to the exact "sweet spot" necessary to accomplish the goals. Horses are very unique, and to perform well they must feel like the job they did was their idea. And this needs to be done in a way to "catch" an elusive steer (the ultimate goal).

One can see how the imagery applies to business. If the leader does not lead, or if the team member does not follow, the elusive goal cannot be obtained. Good cowboys (horsemen) cannot make a horse do anything. First of all, a horse weighs approximately six to seven times the average cowboy's weight. Secondly, horses have minds of their own. Like a good team leader, the horseman must become "one with the horse" and build in a desire by the horse to want to be "joined up" with the rider. In a business with a healthy culture, a great leader is a servant leader. He or she must first become intimately knowledgeable about how their team members think and determine how to get them to be "on the bus." These goals can be accomplished by having healthy business culture, a clear vision, and a great core purpose. The vision and the core purpose must be clearly communicated, so that each team member understands them completely and ultimately buys in. This is the beginning of great business culture.

I think it is clear that the example of team roping can be translated easily to business. It's a wonderful thing to see people work in a harmonious way to accomplish special goals. And this should be a cause to celebrate and sing praise.

CHAPTER 16

FINALLY

Once the leaders and the team members are on the same page, the elusive goals can be accomplished with efficiency and grace. The Ten Commandments and examples of the cowboy code we've discussed in this book all become intimately important to the success of the business, just like the team-roping "run." Let's make a list of these principles and see how each applies:

- Just one God—We must be committed to the vision and "honor" good principles as we honor just one God.
- Honor your team members, just as the cowboy honors his horse and the cattle he is caregiver to.
- No unethical conversation; stay in the "fast lane" of great principles.

- Practice your known core values. Keep the Sunday meeting.
- Put nothing before God. In all things, keep godly principles first.
- No fooling around with unethical behaviors.
- No killing yours or other people's dreams.
- Watch your mouth. Negative emotions or words never work with a horse, and will never be productive with your team members.
- Don't take anything which is not yours—including other people's ideas and aspirations.
- Don't be covetous, especially of other people's success. Rather, learn from what you see and celebrate others' successes.

SUMMARY

In the spring and fall we have the privilege of seeing waves of Canadian geese flying over our ranch. To me personally, it is one of the most awe-inspiring wonders of nature. These majestic birds demonstrate some of the greatest examples of cooperation and selflessness seen in nature. They are not concerned about who's the boss, or about their position in their formation. They take turns leading the way. They create aeronautical advantages for each other by their formation, making their long fall and spring journeys more efficient. They mate for life and are rarely seen quarreling when in flight. They have a mission and clear-cut goals to guide them. They are definitely intentional in all that they do. Their very existence depends on it.

As we have traveled together through this book, I've tried to guide you to a better life of excellence in business by intentional living. The Ten Commandments were our guides to better core business values. I used the great American cowboy as an example of quality living with purpose and intent.

In the Scriptures, the apostle Paul tells us the purpose of the law was to be a schoolmaster, to point out our sin and drive us to Jesus Christ as our Savior (Gal. 3:23–26). What we discover when we try to be perfect in the law is that we fail. Fortunately, we have God's grace and gift of eternal life through Jesus. Jesus paid the price for our mistakes, and gives us an opportunity to be complete in Him.

Cowboys are not all perfect either. Some who read this book might even think of those who have been less then exemplary, and may have even been hurt by a cowboy. This is the nature of man. We are flawed creatures. However, if we live wallowing in our inadequacies or our unforgiveness, we will be living outside of God's will. He died on the cross for us once and for all. He does not need to die over and over.

This is why we must live personally, and, in our businesses, intentionally. If we muddle along by the world's standards and values, we will find misery and failure in the end. If we live intentionally and develop personal and business cultures of excellence based on godly principles, we will be successful no matter what comes our way. To quote a pastor friend: In the scope of eternity, this life we live now is but a "scratch on an endless cable."

If we follow God's values and purposes, life will be richer and more gratifying. I've tried to use the example of the cowboy way to illustrate how we can live a life of thankfulness and integrity, how we can endure hardships and obstacles, how we can be thankful for what we have, how we control our tongues and honor godly values first—how, in the end, it can be said, "well done, good and faithful servant."

AFTERWORD

I owe a great debt of gratitude to the cowboys in my life who have been great mentors. Most of them didn't even know they were mentoring me. So typical of cowboys, they just did what they do, and I was able to observe and learn. Not many people get to live the kind of life I have lived in that regard. I consider these cowboys some of my greatest blessings, for what they taught me and for what I learned about how to do life in a very special way.

The cowboy is a vanishing breed. Modernization has replaced so many of the functions that could only be done by the cowboy in the past. The very nature of these people, however, will never be replaced. They make up a part of the backbone of this great nation we live in.

It would be a great privilege to mention all of their names and thank them for making me a better person. Typical of the cowboys I know, they would be very unhappy to take credit for what they see as their normal lives. They neither brag nor boast, but in my estimation they are heroes in every way. It would be wise to emulate a good cowboy.

The great American cowboy will eventually live on in only myth and legend. However, there are many who are still at work in American ranching and farming communities, throughout the West and other parts of this great land. My hope is that what they stand for will go on to affect many generations to come. We all need heroes, and a cowboy would be a great place to start.

It's been my privilege to work alongside some of the best. I have many memories burned into my mind. Hopefully, I too have had an impact on others to carry on this tradition of living a life with godly character.

For my cowboy friends: Continue to work hard, ride hard, and worship deeply. May God be with you!

ENDNOTES

1. Sanders, J. Oswald, *Spiritual Leadership,* (Chicago: Moody Press, 1994), 80.

2. Ibid., 127, 134.

3. Adams, Ramon F, *The Old-Time Cowhand,* (Lincoln, NE: University of Nebraska Press, 1989), 53.

4. Hunter, J. Marvin, and George W. Saunders, "Courage and Hardiness on the Old Texas Cattle Trail," *The Trail Drivers of Texas,* (San Antonio: Jackson Printing Co., 1920), 110–115.